Success and wealth-building habits: Unveiling the power of consistency and growth

By
William A. Hill

Disclaimer

The information contained within the book is intended for general informational purposes only. The author and publisher have made reasonable efforts to ensure the accuracy and completeness of the content provided in this book; however, they make no representations or warranties of any kind, express or implied, about the accuracy, reliability, suitability, or availability with respect to the information, products, services, or related graphics contained within.

The techniques, strategies, and recommendations presented in this book are based on the author's personal experiences, research, and opinions. Readers are advised to exercise their own judgment and discretion when applying any concepts or practices described in the book. The author and publisher shall not be held liable for any direct, indirect, incidental, consequential, or special damages arising out of the use or misuse of the information provided.

It is important to note that success and wealth-building habits are subjective and may vary depending on individual circumstances, goals, and resources. The book does not guarantee any specific outcomes, financial results, or success. Readers are encouraged to consult with qualified professionals, such as financial advisors or experts in relevant fields, for personalized advice tailored to their specific needs and objectives.

The author and publisher disclaim any responsibility for any loss or damage to individuals or organizations arising directly or indirectly from the use or application of the information presented in this book. The inclusion of any third-party resources, websites, or references does not imply endorsement or responsibility for their content or services.

Every effort has been made to respect copyright laws and acknowledge the sources of information used in this book. If any material has been used inadvertently without permission or proper attribution, the author and publisher will be pleased to make the necessary corrections in subsequent editions or printings.

By reading this book, readers acknowledge and agree to the above disclaimer and accept full responsibility for their actions and decisions based on the information provided.

Table of Content

Introduction

In a world driven by ambition and dreams of financial prosperity, the pursuit of success and wealth-building has become a significant focus for many individuals. In the book "Success and Wealth-Building Habits: Releasing the Power of Consistency and Growth," we delve into the transformative journey towards achieving prosperity and uncovering the key habits that pave the path to enduring success.

This book serves as a practical guide, illuminating the power of consistency and growth in the pursuit of success and wealth. It is designed to equip readers with essential insights and strategies that have the potential to revolutionize their mind-set, habits, and approach to creating lasting financial abundance.

Drawing upon extensive research, real-life case studies, and personal experiences, "Success and Wealth-Building Habits" provides a comprehensive framework that explores the interplay between consistency, growth, and the creation of sustainable wealth. This book aims to empower readers to harness their potential, unlock hidden opportunities, and forge a new path towards a future of prosperity.

Through the pages of this book, readers will gain a deeper understanding of the habits that successful individuals have cultivated and leveraged to build enduring wealth. By unravelling the principles that underpin their achievements, readers can apply these insights to their own lives and embark on a transformative journey towards realizing their aspirations.

Join us on this enlightening exploration of success and wealth-building habits, as we embark on a compelling journey towards unlocking the true potential within ourselves and unleashing the power of consistency and growth. Get ready to embark on a transformative experience that will guide you towards creating the life of abundance you deserve.

CHAPTER ONE

The habits of the successful and wealthy

Why are some people more successful than the others? you see you don't decide your future you decide your habits and your habits decide your future no one succeeds overnight and no one fails overnight, success is nothing more than some of small efforts repeated day in and day out today I want to share with you the 10 successful habits that I have learned and developed over the years.

Habit number one: accept complete responsibility for your own life

People that are successful assume full accountability for their own lives. You know, I was struggling in my 20s, I had just closed my 13th business that I had started and failed at 13, and I was then confused and I was blaming I was blaming everyone else when I met my first mentor Allen, when he sat me down and he asked me this question, "What's not working"? I complained that nothing was going right, that I wasn't making enough money, that I was in debt, and that I couldn't figure out why I kept having failures. Customers are so cheap, I don't see why taxes and other fees are so high, the economy is poor, and I was simply blaming everyone. I wasn't accepting full responsibility for my life, and my mentor Allen told me that I wouldn't succeed unless I did. I thought, "Maybe he's right;" at the time, I thought, "Maybe not entirely, but perhaps I'm at fault," and he responded, "Maybe not;" you chose to stop those businesses, choose those partners, and spend your time on this; every single decision you made on your own went to the passive knowledge, but you still chose what happened, you chose, and you acted on it. From that point on, I learned to accept responsibility; the onus is always on me. You need to consider this since lazy individuals like to place blame on others. You can either earn money or produce results, but not both. Therefore, habit number one is to assume full responsibility for your life.

Habit number two: You must determine your particular goals.

The reason why most people in life don't get what they want is that they are unsure of what they want. When I told my mentor that I hadn't set any goals up to that point, he advised me to do so. What do you really want? When I was younger, I believed that my ambition was to own the RX8 Master Red Rotary Engine. I thought if I could get that car I would have made it right there was my dream there was my only dream but I thought it would be so cool if I could drive that car and he said good said that's a goal make that, that's what you want to do right?, okay great so now from kind of like you know I'm doing all these things and I'm starting all these businesses and I wanted to provide for my mom but I needed something to motivate myself, I needed something I could see and feel that I could simply focus on, and the RX8 was great for me because I was driving the Hatchback Mazda 3 at the time and wanted to upgrade; it was my goal. So habit number two is to know exactly what you want, and once you know exactly what you want.

Habit number three: You must believe it is feasible.

You must believe it is feasible. That's all there is to it; you simply have to believe that it is feasible not only for others but also for yourself. Now, because I was already driving the Mazda 3, it wasn't like I was hoping to get a Lamborghini or a Ferrari at the time. Okay, it's an enhancement, I thought, if I could only concentrate, it might be doable for me, and it wouldn't feel so far-fetched. it doesn't seem like you're not living in the basement with your mom and now you want to buy a $10 million home it was like hey I'm driving a hatchback and I could upgrade to a sports car that was it so you have to believe it's possible it's possible for you Napoleon Hill talks about this in thinking grow rich whatever your mind can conceive and believe you can achieve and it's very true.

Habit number four: Highly successful individuals envision success.

Highly successful individuals imagine success, so here's what I did after I realized this was my goal: I took 100 percent responsibility for making it happen, and I think I can make it happen. I visualize success, so I grabbed a page from a magazine with the RX8 on it and pinned it to my vision board. I will look at it every day and imagine what it looks like right now. I could see my hands right here, I could see the stick right there, I could see the whole car and see the interior I could feel that let us sit and I would visualize and visualize and visualize until it became so vivid in my mind that I could see it, I could smell it, I could feel it right, I could feel that I deserve this, this is what I could do and I do that every day visualize my success.

Habit number five People who are successful act as if they are.

When I hang out with my friends, sometimes we'll see an RX8 driving by, and I'll say, "Hey, that's my car right there." They'll reply, "You're crazy, what are you talking about, that's not your car," to which I reply, "That's my car, no you drive the hatchback," so "no that is my car." However, every time I see the RX8, I'm conditioning myself to believe that the result has already been achieved, Most people wait until they see the outcome before saying, "Oh yeah, then they feel like they deserve it." No, you have to believe that you deserve it first before the result will come along.

Habit number 6 People who are successful are willing to pay the price.

Successful individuals are willing to pay the price. It's one thing to dream and another to believe, but at the end of the day, you have to do something right and be willing to pay the price, which in this case is very easy to calculate because it's simply a car. So I found out exactly and precisely how much this automobile is going to cost me, and I thought to myself, okay, it's going to cost me this much in down payment, this much in monthly payment.

Okay, so what I needed to do was focus on generating enough income to pay for that, and I was willing to pay the price, so when my friends were going to pubs, partying, or just wasting time, I was working. I was working day in and day out, no breaks, no time off.

I would just concentrate because I was willing to pay the price for achievement, therefore one of the things you must ask yourself is what price you are willing to pay for success. What are you willing to give up, what are you willing to sacrifice, since there is always a trade off?

Habit number seven Successful people experience dread, but they nevertheless take action.

Successful people are afraid, but they do it regardless since many people believe that successful people have no fears. Of course, we have concerns, doubts, and are apprehensive about making a decision. We are human at times, but the difference is that we do not allow fear stop us, we don't allow fear dictate who we are or what we will not do; we feel the dread, you feel the fear, but we do it anyhow, and remember, I need to pick up the phone. I had to phone business owners in order to get clients. Was I scared? You bet you. Was I worried? You bet you. Do their rejections appeal to me? No way, no how. But I sense the terror and go nevertheless; just keep going!! Keep going!!! And you keep going.

Habit number Eight: Successful individuals look for mentoring.

People who are successful desire mentorship. You see unsuccessful people very often they have a big ego and please listen to me, your ego is not your amigo. Your ego is not your friend; in fact, it will ruin you. See, when I was doing things my way, I allowed my ego keep me from seeking mentorship until I discovered my first mentor.

Now, that may or may not be the solution for everyone, but it was the answer for me in terms of finding my mentor, finding that first mentor who changed my life and turned my life around, and pursuing mentorship.

I don't have all the answers, I don't know everything, and the more you learn, the more you realize how little you know, so my mentor was teaching me the mentality and skill set that I needed to reach my goals of purchasing an RX8, Does it mean I don't have failures? Of course I do, but success is moving from failure to failure without losing enthusiasm.

Habit number nine People who are successful are enthusiastic.

You'll observe that high-income people have a lot of energy, whereas low-income folks have no energy, can't get anything done, aren't productive, can't make it happen, and lack vitality. The drive, the excitement, and the stamina to make things happen and how are you going to accomplish anything if you don't approach it with passion and enthusiasm? You may not be the best at it right now, but if you're enthusiastic and believe in your passion and are incredibly passionate about what you do, you'll make it happen, so that's a very important habit that leads to the last habit.

Habit number 10 Successful people are dedicated to continuous improvement.

Successful people are dedicated to continuous improvement. After all of this, I act as if I've paid the price, and I seek mentorship. I kept going till I eventually acquired the automobile, and I was so excited that I went to the showroom, where I had already cast drove the car several times.

I knew exactly what I was getting myself into when I came into the news show and the car salesperson told me he had never sold a car this quickly. We got the paperwork done, I drove the car off the lot, and what's intriguing is that I felt it was great straight away.

and I was driving the car right out of the parking lot and you know how I felt peace I felt that I've seen this I've experienced this many times I felt that just like it you know what this is this is my car because I visualize it so many times I was actually incredibly calm this is how it's supposed to be and that's great because I'd seen it in my mind so many times, I acted as if I knew it was mine, and when it was mine, it was a big deal right? Then I set the next goal, I want to get the next car, and I know at the time I thought car was my thing, I'm not interested in those things anymore by the time I thought I'll get a next car, a Mercedes, an Audi 8, and so on and so forth. So successful people seek mentorship; they also never stop developing; it's always about becoming a better version of yourself. If you want to be healthier, you'll study diet and exercise, right? If you wish to be an excellent cook, you will learn recipes from auto sheriffs and bring some ideas with you. It's not any different If you want to be successful, you have to make that a subject that you study, something that you take seriously, something that you put effort into, so which one of these successful habits you are going to implement, maybe not all of them at once, but what is that one habit that you want to implement today?

CHAPTER TWO

Breaking free from the 9-to-5 mind-set

The only two reasons you should work a 9 to 5 job are that you can only earn so much money and that you will always be dependent on one source of income. You must even seek permission from your supervisor to take a day off. Working a 9 to 5 job will never completely liberate you. However, there are only two reasons why you should work from 9 a.m. until 5 p.m.

The first is that you enjoy doing it. I don't mean that you get to challenge yourself and that the pace is normally moderate; rather, there is nothing I would rather do than this type of work. The only other reason to work 9 to 5 is to use it as a stepping stone to independence, to develop your talents and learn on the job so you may someday start freelancing or even starting your own business while working 9 to 5. You're working on side projects and side hustles; there's no reason for you to work 9 to 5.

Break free from the notion that success is a four-letter word that you must endure because it leaves you with a bad taste in your mouth. Focus on what you do best and what you enjoy to produce results that matter to you. That's how we succeed. We start to see things we've never seen before, and we start to believe that we can achieve our goals.

By setting your financial objectives and examining your current situation, you can begin to realize the financial freedom you've been seeking and create a life of flexibility and prosperity. Make a plan, prioritize your own development, and continue to study personal finance.

Living within your means and making sensible financial decisions will help you get closer to financial independence. Break free from the standard 9 to 5 work model and take charge of your finances to create a life of freedom. With tenacity, prioritize personal improvement and many sources of revenue. Using a strategic approach, you may achieve financial independence and design a life on your own terms. Remember, financial freedom is within your grasp. Begin today and take the first steps toward creating the life you want.

Breaking Free from the 9-to-5 Mindset: Embracing a New Paradigm of Work-Life Balance

The traditional 9-to-5 work schedule has long been ingrained in our society as the standard for employment. However, as our lives become more complex and our priorities shift, many individuals are seeking alternatives to break free from the constraints of this mindset. In this essay, we will explore the concept of breaking free from the 9-to-5 mindset, the advantages it offers, and strategies to embrace a new paradigm of work-life balance.

1. Rethinking Work-Life Balance

The 9-to-5 mindset often perpetuates a strict separation between work and personal life. However, achieving true work-life balance requires a shift in perspective. It involves recognizing that work is not the sole defining aspect of our lives and that personal fulfillment and well-being should also be prioritized. By redefining work-life balance, we can create a more holistic approach that integrates our passions, relationships, and personal growth alongside our professional pursuits.

2. Embracing Flexibility and Remote Work

Breaking free from the 9-to-5 mindset opens doors to embrace flexibility and remote work opportunities. Advancements in technology have made it possible for many professions to be performed remotely or with flexible schedules. This freedom allows individuals to tailor their work hours to suit their personal needs, enabling a better integration of work and personal life. Embracing flexibility and remote work empowers individuals to take control of their schedules and optimize productivity while maintaining a healthy work-life balance.

3. Pursuing Entrepreneurship and Freelancing

One way to escape the 9-to-5 mindset is by pursuing entrepreneurship or freelancing. Building a business or working as a freelancer offers the freedom to create one's own schedule, choose projects that align with personal values, and explore new opportunities. While this path may require additional effort and risk-taking, it provides the potential for increased autonomy, fulfillment, and financial rewards. Embracing an entrepreneurial mindset allows individuals to shape their own career paths and find a balance that suits their unique circumstances.

4. Prioritizing Personal Growth and Well-being

Breaking free from the 9-to-5 mindset involves prioritizing personal growth and well-being. This shift acknowledges that professional success is not the sole measure of a fulfilling life. It involves dedicating time and energy to activities that promote physical health, mental well-being, and personal interests. By prioritizing self-care, pursuing hobbies, and investing in personal development, individuals can create a more balanced and fulfilling life that extends beyond the confines of traditional work hours.

5. Cultivating a Mindset of Purpose and Meaning.

Escaping the 9-to-5 mindset requires cultivating a mindset of purpose and meaning. It involves aligning professional endeavors with personal values and passions. By seeking work that provides a sense of purpose and contributes to the greater good, individuals can find deeper satisfaction and fulfillment in their careers. This mindset shift allows individuals to view work as an avenue for personal growth and impact, rather than merely a means of earning a paycheck.

Breaking free from the 9-to-5 mindset is a transformative journey that offers numerous benefits. By redefining work-life balance, embracing flexibility and remote work, pursuing entrepreneurship, prioritizing personal growth and well-being, and cultivating a mindset of purpose and meaning, individuals can create a more harmonious and fulfilling life. It is important to remember that each person's path may differ, and it requires self-reflection and deliberate choices. Embracing this new paradigm allows individuals to design a life that aligns with their values, aspirations, and desired work-life balance.

CHAPTER THREE

Laying the groundwork: tiny changes, big results

Small changes that makes big impact, successful people are simply those with successful habits. Did you know that research in the field of psychology has shown us that 95% of everything that we think we do and achieve is the result of habit? there's no denying that our habits exhibit an enormous amount of influence in our lives but what if you were able to control which habits you adopted and which ones you left behind it turns out that controlling your habits is a lot easier than you might realise and doing so is a powerful way to make impactful changes in your life, if you want to form a new habit follow these 7 steps.

First, make a decision.

the first step to forming a new habit is to decide which habit you would like to adopt examine your goals and determine which habits might help you reach them for example if your goal is to become more informed about world events heading into the habit of reading the newspaper every morning is one option to consider whatever your goals might be highlight the positive habits that will help you along the way and commit to making those habits a part of your regular routine.

The Art of Decision-Making: A Path to Success

Throughout life, we are faced with countless decisions that shape our present and future. Making informed and effective decisions is a skill that can greatly influence our personal and professional lives. In this essay, we will explore the process of decision-making, discuss key factors to consider, and highlight the importance of thoughtful deliberation in achieving favourable outcomes.

The first step in making a decision is to clearly define the problem or situation at hand. Understanding the nature and scope of the decision allows for a focused approach. It is important to identify the desired outcome and consider any potential constraints or challenges that may impact the decision-making process. By defining the decision, we establish a framework for evaluation and analysis.

Informed decisions require adequate information. Collecting relevant and reliable data is essential to understand the various aspects and potential consequences of the decision. This involves conducting research, seeking expert opinions, and considering past experiences or case studies. Gathering information broadens our perspective and enables us to make more informed choices.

Once the necessary information is gathered, it is crucial to evaluate available alternatives. This involves generating potential solutions or courses of action that could address the defined problem or situation. Each alternative should be carefully examined, considering its feasibility, potential outcomes, risks, and benefits. By assessing various options, we increase the likelihood of identifying the most favourable path forward.

Decisions are not solely based on rationality; they are also influenced by our values and priorities. It is important to reflect on personal or organizational values and how they align with the potential outcomes of each alternative. Considering our priorities ensures that the decision aligns with our long-term goals and aspirations, contributing to a sense of fulfilment and satisfaction.

An effective decision requires a thorough analysis of the pros and cons associated with each alternative. Weighing the potential benefits against the risks and drawbacks provides a balanced perspective. By evaluating the potential outcomes and their impact, we can make decisions that maximize benefits while mitigating potential negative consequences.

While rational analysis is essential, intuition also plays a role in decision-making. Our subconscious mind often considers factors that are not immediately apparent. Trusting our intuition can provide valuable insights and guide us towards the most suitable choice. Intuition, when combined with informed analysis, can lead to innovative and successful decisions.

Making decisions is an integral part of life. By following a systematic approach that involves defining the decision, gathering information, evaluating alternatives, considering values and priorities, weighing pros and cons, and trusting our intuition, we enhance our decision-making skills. Effective decision-making empowers us to navigate challenges, seize opportunities, and achieve our goals. With practice and reflection, we can refine this skill and pave our path to success.

The second stage is to avoid making exceptions.

nothing kills the process of forming a beneficial habit faster than allowing yourself exceptions the problem with exceptions is that they tend to snowball one excuse turns into another until you've come up with more reasons to avoid your new habit than reasons to pursue it if you want to form a habit that actually sticks you'll need to avoid all exceptions and excuses that might cross your mind.

Avoiding Exceptions is also a Key to Consistency and Fairness which are essential principles in various aspects of life, whether personal or professional. Making exceptions, however, can undermine these principles and lead to dissatisfaction and inequality. In this essay, we will explore the importance of avoiding exceptions and discuss practical strategies to ensure consistency and fairness in decision-making processes.

Understanding the consequences of exceptions, making exceptions can have significant repercussions on individuals and organizations. When exceptions are made, it creates an imbalance in the application of rules or policies, leading to feelings of favouritism or unfair treatment. Exceptions erode trust, as people may perceive the decision-making process as arbitrary or inconsistent. Additionally, exceptions can establish a precedent, making it more challenging to maintain standards and expectations in the future. It is crucial to recognize the potential harm that exceptions can cause and strive for a more equitable approach.

Clarify and Communicate Guidelines to avoid making exceptions, it is vital to establish clear guidelines and communicate them effectively. By outlining specific criteria or rules, everyone involved understands the expectations and can adhere to them consistently. When guidelines are ambiguous or open to interpretation, it increases the likelihood of exceptions being made. Effective communication ensures that all individuals are aware of the guidelines and can provide input or seek clarification when needed. Transparency is key to fostering a culture of fairness and reducing the temptation to make exceptions.

Implement Objective Decision-Making Processes Subjectivity often leads to exceptions. To mitigate this, objective decision-making processes should be implemented. By basing decisions on measurable and verifiable criteria, the risk of personal biases or favouritism influencing outcomes is minimized. Objective processes can include the use of standardized assessments, performance metrics, or predetermined evaluation methods. These approaches provide a solid foundation for consistent decision-making and reduce the likelihood of exceptions based on personal opinions or preferences.

Consider Precedents and Precedence, when faced with a situation that seems to warrant an exception, it is essential to consider precedents and the concept of precedence. Reflect on past decisions and their outcomes to determine if similar circumstances have been previously addressed and how they were handled. Evaluating precedents helps establish a framework for consistency and can guide decision-making without resorting to exceptions. By adhering to established patterns, individuals and organizations uphold fairness and ensure that similar situations are treated consistently.

Seek Alternative Solutions, Instead of making exceptions, explore alternative solutions that align with established guidelines. If a particular situation seems to warrant an exception, consider whether there are other options available that can address the underlying issue while still adhering to the rules or policies in place. Collaborative problem-solving and creativity can often lead to innovative solutions that avoid exceptions altogether. By actively seeking alternatives, we can maintain consistency and fairness while addressing unique circumstances.

Consistency and fairness are crucial for maintaining trust and fostering a positive environment in various spheres of life. Avoiding exceptions is an essential aspect of upholding these principles. By understanding the consequences, clarifying guidelines, implementing objective decision-making processes, considering precedents, and seeking alternative solutions, we can create a more equitable and consistent world.

Third, inform people about your new habit.

when you tell people that you are close to that you are trying to form a certain habit it adds a degree of social pressure to your motivating factors no one wants to be seen publicly falling short of their goals so letting others know about the goals that you are pursuing is 1 great way to keep yourself on track and motivated when you discuss your new habit with close friends or family they can help hold you accountable next make you some visualisation. visualisation techniques are incredibly beneficial for helping people achieve a wide range of goals including the goal of forming a new habit every day try to visualise what your life would be like if you fully adopted the habit that you're pursuing what positive changes can you visualise this habit breathing how in adopting this new habit make you feel if you can visualise the answer to questions such as these then you are sure to find staying committed to your new habit that much easier.

The fifth step is to write a positive affirmation.

Like visualisation techniques positive affirmations are a mental tool that can go a long way towards helping you form a beneficial new habits. For example if your goal is to get into the habit of going on a run every morning, the affirmation you repeat to yourself each and every day might sound something like this I am going to be the healthiest and happiest version of myself and running will help me reach that goal while it may feel a little silly at first constantly repeating these affirmations to yourself there is no denying the science behind their effectiveness at requiring a person's mentality over time.

Number six resolved to persevere.

The best thing about forming a beneficial habit is that once it truly becomes a habit performing whatever behaviour you wanted to adopt will become second nature something that you do without even thinking about it getting to this point however takes time and you must resolve to persist and overcome obstacles until your new habit is fully cemented into your daily routine.

Seventh, give yourself a reward.

Each time you perform the habit that you're trying to adopt give yourself a small reward for instance if your goal is to start reading more in the afternoons you might consider rewarding yourself with a small treat such as a piece of candy each time you hit a certain milestone such as finishing a chapter in the book that you're reading these small rewards might not seem like much but activating the rewards under your brain and associating it with the new habit that you are trying to form is something that has been proven to have powerful results.

CHAPTER FOUR

Developing a success mind-set

Develop a success mentality is a great approach to accelerate your personal and professional development. It entails taking a proactive and optimistic approach to life, making significant goals, and cultivating habits that aid in your success. Here are a few basic tactics for cultivating a success mind-set:

Establish Specific Goals: Clearly define what success means to you. Set measurable goals that reflect your values and desires. To keep focused and motivated, break things down into smaller, doable tasks.

Develop a good Attitude: Develop a good attitude by focusing on possibilities rather than problems. Accept adversities as learning opportunities and retain a positive attitude. Avoid negative self-talk by surrounding oneself with positive influences.

Value progress and Learning: View setbacks as chances for progress. Consider failures to be valuable lessons and modify your strategy accordingly. Continuously seek knowledge, learn new skills, and be receptive to critique. Adopting a growth mind-set enables you to adapt and thrive in changing circumstances.

Accept Responsibility: Take responsibility for your actions and outcomes. Avoid blaming people or making excuses. Recognize that you have power over your choices and responses. Accepting responsibility allows you to make great changes and move forward.

Build Resilience: Resilience is critical for success. Develop mental and emotional fortitude to recover from failures. Maintain perspective, take care of yourself, and create a support network. You can endure through setbacks and stay focused on your goals if you develop resilience.

Develop Self-Discipline: Develop self-discipline to stay devoted to your goals. Set priorities, manage your time properly, and avoid distractions. Create everyday behaviours that are congruent with your vision of success.

Seek Inspiration and Motivation: Surround yourself with motivators and role models. Read books, listen to podcasts, or attend seminars that are relevant to your interests and goals. Find inspiration in other people's success stories and utilize them to drive your own quest.

Accept Failure as Feedback: Rather than dreading failure, view it as an opportunity for growth. Learn from your mistakes, make changes, and keep going. Recognize that failure is a natural part of the route to achievement, and that each setback takes you closer to your objectives.

Practice Gratitude: Develop a grateful attitude for what you have and the progress you've achieved. Focus on the positive aspects of your life and enjoy your accomplishments, no matter how modest. Gratitude promotes a positive outlook and brings greater success into your life.

Take Action: Having a success mind-set entails more than just thinking positively; it also entails taking consistent action toward your goals. Break free from procrastination, conquer self-doubt, and step outside your comfort zone. Develop an action bias and keep going forward.

Create a Positive Environment: Surround yourself with people that inspire and motivate you. Seek for mentors, join professional networks, or participate in communities where you can share ideas and get help. A good and supportive atmosphere may help you flourish while also holding you accountable.

Visualize Success: Visualize your desired outcome in detail. Visualize yourself reaching your objectives and feeling successful. Revisit this visualization on a regular basis to boost your motivation and confidence in your capacity to accomplish.

Practice Self-Care: It is critical to take care of your physical and mental well-being in order to retain a success mentality. Make self-care activities such as exercise, appropriate diet, adequate sleep, and stress-reduction techniques a priority. When you prioritize your health, you have the energy and concentration to achieve your goals.

Embrace Risk and Adaptability: Success frequently entails taking measured chances and being adaptable. Accept unpredictability and be willing to venture outside of your comfort zone. Adaptability enables you to overcome obstacles and capitalize on possibilities.

Study the Habits, techniques, and Mind-sets of Successful People: Research the habits, techniques, and mind-sets of successful people in your sector or industry. Read biographies, listen to interviews, or go to conferences to learn from others' experiences. Apply the lessons you learn from their experiences to your own road to success.

Celebrate Progress: Recognize and celebrate your accomplishments along the road. Recognize your progress, even if it isn't yet your final aim. Celebrating accomplishments builds confidence, encourages positive behaviour, and provides incentive to keep going.

Mindfulness Practice: Practice mindfulness by remaining present in the moment and completely engaging in your tasks. Reduce stress and enhance focus by using mindfulness techniques such as meditation or deep breathing exercises. Being present allows you to make better judgments and increase your productivity.

Evaluate and Adjust Continually: Regularly analyse your progress and think on what is working and what needs to be improved. Adjust your strategies as needed to match with your objectives. To increase your chances of success, be adaptable and willing to change your strategy.

Seek Feedback and Learn from Failure: Seek feedback actively from trusted mentors, colleagues, or coaches.

Constructive feedback provides important insights for growth and development. Consider failure as an opportunity to learn and adapt your strategy accordingly.

Practice Persistence and Perseverance: Success does not usually happen overnight. Maintain a strong work ethic even when confronted with difficulties or disappointments. Regardless of the challenges, stay focused on your long-term vision and keep moving forward. Persistence and perseverance are essential factors for long-term success.

Remember that cultivating a success mentality is an ongoing process that necessitates consistent effort and a dedication to personal development. You may create a mind-set that propels you toward success in all areas of your life by adopting these tactics into your life and maintaining a positive, proactive attitude. Creating a success mentality is a journey that takes continual effort and introspection. Adopting these tactics and remaining persistent will allow you to realize your full potential and achieve the success you seek.

CHAPTER FIVE

Consistency is a powerful tool

When it comes to establishing success, the importance of consistency cannot be overstated. Consistency is the act of consistently showing up and doing action over time, even when faced with hurdles or diversions. It is your consistent dedication to your goals and your steadfast commitment to carrying out your plans. Here's why consistency is so effective:

Builds Momentum: Consistency in your efforts builds momentum. When you take action on a constant basis, even if it is in small steps, you develop a sense of progress and forward motion. Each action builds on the one before it, generating momentum that pulls you closer to your objectives.

Fosters Discipline: Consistency fosters discipline. You build your self-discipline muscles by committing to a regular regimen or practice. It becomes simpler to reject temptations, overcome procrastination, and stay focused on what genuinely important. Discipline is a major characteristic of successful people, and consistency is the method to gaining it.

Establishes Trust and Reliability: Consistency fosters trust and reliability in both yourself and others. People believe you will follow through if you consistently deliver on your promises. This strengthens relationships, whether personal or professional, and opens the door to new chances.

Forms Habits: The foundation of habit formation is consistency. When you perform an action or behaviours on a regular basis, it becomes embedded in your routine and becomes a habit. Positive habits are effective because they automate activities that contribute to your success. You will almost certainly make progress if you continuously practice these practices.

Overcomes Resistance: Consistency assists you in overcoming resistance and overcoming challenges. It is inevitable to encounter difficulties and failures along the way. However, by continually taking action and remaining engaged, you may build resilience and perseverance. Consistency allows you to navigate challenging situations and emerge stronger on the other side.

Increases Efficiency and Productivity: Consistency increases efficiency and productivity. When you stick to a schedule, you avoid decision fatigue and improve your workflow. Because your activities become automatic, you no longer waste time pondering about what to do next. This helps you to concentrate your efforts on higher-level tasks and accomplish more in less time.

Shows Commitment: Consistency demonstrates your dedication to your aims and desires. It sends a strong statement that you are committed to your personal development and achievement. This commitment not only inspires and motivates you, but also people around you. Individuals who display constant dedication are more likely to receive assistance and collaboration.

Produces Results: In the end, consistency produces results. Success is rarely the result of a single spectacular gesture; rather, it is the result of sustained effort over time. By persistently working toward your goals, you increase your chances of success. Every step forward, no matter how tiny, puts you closer to your goal.

It's critical to establish a routine, hold yourself accountable, and set clear goals if you want to harness the power of consistency. Make a commitment to taking persistent action toward your goals by breaking them down into manageable activities. Keep in mind that consistency is about constantly showing up and making improvement rather than about being perfect. Accept the power of consistency, and you'll see how it can completely change the course of your success.

We must all suffer one of two things: the pain of consistency or the pain of regret or disappointment. Your choices will determine what you will be in the future. Most people unknowingly choose the pain of regret or disappointment because they are inconsistent and give up on their goals. They will always look for an easy path, Goals of the road to achievement cannot be attained without discipline and consistency, as Daniel Washington once observed. Consistency is the bridge that connects goals and accomplishment, while ambition is the road to success. One of the essential components of success in every field of life is consistency. Without consistency, sustained progress is impossible, and without consistency, success is absent. The achievement of goals requires constancy. As Napoleon Hill once stated, without consistency, dreams cannot become realities. Haitians' tenacity and perseverance are an unbeatable combination for success. Success doesn't come from doing great things or taking big steps; rather, it comes from consistently doing small things over and over until you achieve overnight success. You have to keep moving, no matter what attitude you have, to remain consistent in every situation, consistent in your dream consistent in your goal, majority of individuals say, I tried my best, but it didn't work out. I would say What most people actually do, in my opinion, is go to the gym on the first, second, or third day; they begin reading their first book even if they only get through the first few pages; however, they give up after a few days or stop going altogether because they did not see any progress; almost everyone starts. almost every people knock on the door of their dream once but only a few of them keep knocking on that door because most of the people run away before anyone has a chance to open that door but if you keep knocking persistently and endlessly eventually the door will obey so today I want to stay away to five lessons on the power of consistent 5 reasons why you must be consistent to achieve your goals and dreams

Number one

Pain today, tears tomorrow Some people believe that being strong means never feeling pain, but in reality, the strongest people are those who feel it, understand it, accept it, and keep going anyway. It's not what we do once in a while that saves our lives; it's what we do consistently. Most people quit because of pain; most people fail to work consistently because pain is temporary and even truly it will subside. You must ask yourself, "Am I willing to sacrifice today in order to achieve the results I desire in the future?" It's about having the fortitude to say yes when you want to give up; it's about having the courage to say, "I'm willing to sacrifice for my future." Please choose the pain that provides you the long-term game over the agony that offers you the short-term game. Nobody went anyplace significant in life without cultivating amazing constancy. Nobody on this earth has ever reached significant heights without being consistent. If you are not willing to make sacrifices now in order to have that pride tomorrow, you will never have it. There is no gain without suffering, and there is no consistency without success. You may be tempted to quit now because of the short campaign, but what will you say when you look in the mirror? What will you say when people ask you who you are and what you have done in life? What will you feel then remember there is no better feeling than looking in the mirror and saying I built this, I created this, I sacrificed for this, I worked for this, and I am proud of this. Do not give up, and do not let the suffering go. The pain is not stronger than you; you are stronger than it. Do not choose the easy route; if he does, your life will be difficult in the future. It's all about those small decisions you make every day. Be strong today so that you can be proud tomorrow. Be strong today so that you can be stronger tomorrow. Be consistent today so that you can be proud tomorrow. Be consistent today so that you can be stronger tomorrow.

Number Two

Remember why you store it giving up is the most common decision when successful people most people quit after working some days because they didn't see and result and they didn't see any result because they didn't work consistently they give up because their power consistent is very low he must be consistent on your dreams by facing the pain or by weaning over the pain so when you feel like quitting remember pain is temporary and greatness lasts forever when you feel like quitting remember why you started push through the pain don't let it stop you pause it to grow you whatever is happening in your life will make it through the pain whatever struggle that you're facing you can make the change remember those who said you feel and let that fuel your flame you might be down today but you are not the same.

Number Three

motivation does not last so you must be consistent you won't always be motivated so you must learn to be consistent motivation does not last for a long time there is a difference between motivated people and consistent people motivated people at some point somehow will give up but a consistent people will never ever give up because consistent people are always focused on the end result they start at the end and figure out how to get there from where they are but motivated people focus on where they are and how hard it is right now so they think they will do everything today they always looking forward to make it so quick and at some point they will lose their motivation and will give up so be consistent cause great things take time so your power of consistency as every to the said no great thing is created solidly Jack can feel said everything valuable takes time I know overnight success

Number Four

one day at a time keep going is the most powerful attitude of a successful people I inspired by a code of team peerless day by day one day at a time I will be closer step by step 1 step at a time I will be closer choice by choice 1 choice at a time I will be better successful people are consistent they more step by step they do not go heavy to think they do not take pressures that I have to do a lot of work today they just simply know one thing that they have to take a little step today just one little step and feel that I have built this I have done this I have created this when you have a great and difficult task something perhaps almost impossible if you only work a little at a time every day a little suddenly that work will finish itself as Vincent van Gogh said great things are not done while you pause but my series of small things brought together as Robert Clayer said success is the sum of the small efforts repeated day in and day out.

Number Five

Two minutes every day do not underestimate the power of two minutes or little stay you have no idea what a day two minutes can do for you, you know almost every people are ready to take action on their goals they thought it takes a big step more time and hard work they think they will do more and more or everything today but next day they stop showing up too many stuff in the accent daily is more harder than 2 hours of one day training because too many sub daily accident needs you to be consistent to make the quickest progress you don't have to take huge leaves you just have to take baby steps and keep on taking them two minutes every day and let's see what happens in your life

CHAPTER SIX

Networking and relationship building

Personal and professional success require the ability to network and develop relationships. Building a strong network and cultivating meaningful relationships can lead to new opportunities, support and mentorship, and overall growth. Here are some major networking and relationship-building strategies:

Be Genuine and Authentic: Approach networking and connection development with a genuine desire to connect and build mutually beneficial partnerships. People are more likely to connect with and trust those who are sincere and true to themselves.

Expand Your Network: Seek out ways to broaden your network. Attend trade shows, seminars, and networking events. Join professional organizations or groups in your subject of interest. Connect with like-minded professionals by using internet platforms such as LinkedIn. Be willing to meet new individuals from various backgrounds and businesses.

Practice Active Listening: Engage in active listening throughout conversations. Pay complete attention to the person with whom you are conversing. Ask pertinent questions and allow them to share their experiences and insights to demonstrate genuine interest. Active listening fosters a stronger relationship and demonstrates that you value their viewpoint.

Provide Value: Networking is about more than just what you can get; it's also about what you can give. Find methods to add value to others without expecting immediate gratification. Share your experience, information, or resources. When needed, provide assistance or support. You create trust and goodwill within your network by being helpful and generous.

Follow Up and Stay in Touch: After your initial encounters, follow up with the people you meet to keep the connection going. Send individual messages of thanks for the talk and any insights gleaned. Keep in touch on a regular basis by sharing pertinent articles, updates, or congratulating them on their accomplishments. Regular communication strengthens the bond and keeps you on their mind.

Seek Mentorship: Locate people in your field who have attained the degree of achievement you desire. Reach out to them and convey your appreciation for their work. Seek their advice and mentoring. A mentor can help you manage your career or personal growth by providing useful insights, advice, and support.

Build Reciprocity: Reciprocity is the foundation of all relationships. Be willing to help and encourage others in their endeavours. Seek out possibilities to assist them in achieving their objectives. They are more inclined to reciprocate when you continually display your eagerness to contribute to their success.

Embrace Diversity and Inclusion: Work to create a network that is both varied and inclusive. Connect with people from all backgrounds, cultures, and opinions. Diversity broadens your network by introducing new ideas and opportunities. Accept inclusivity and cultivate an environment in which everyone feels welcome and appreciated.

Attend Informal Gatherings: Don't confine your networking to formal gatherings. Meet-ups, social groups, and informal get-togethers can all provide excellent networking possibilities. These easy going settings promote the formation of more honest and deeper interactions.

Maintain Professionalism and Integrity: In all your dealings, maintain professionalism and integrity. Maintain respect, dependability, and confidentiality when necessary. Developing a reputation as someone who conducts with honesty and professionalism boosts trust and improves connections.

Use Social Media to establish Relationships: Use social media platforms to grow your network and establish relationships. Participate in industry-related discussions, share useful knowledge, and network with professionals in your sector. Participate actively in online networks and groups to develop your presence and network with like-minded people.

Attend Professional Development Events: Attend workshops, seminars, and conferences that are relevant to your industry or areas of interest. These events allow you to network with professionals who have similar goals and interests. Engage in conversations, ask questions, and exchange contact information to continue the dialogue after the event.

Volunteer and Give Back: Engaging in volunteer work not only contributes to a cause you care about but also allows you to network with individuals who share your passion. Participate in community service projects, join non-profit organizations, or offer your expertise to help others. Volunteering can lead to meaningful connections and a sense of fulfilment.

Be a Connector: Act as a connector within your network by introducing individuals who can benefit from knowing each other. Be proactive in connecting people with similar interests or complementary skills. By facilitating connections, you position yourself as a valuable resource and strengthen your network.

Show Gratitude and Appreciation: Express gratitude and appreciation for the support and assistance you receive from your network. Send thank-you notes or emails to acknowledge the contributions of others. Showing genuine appreciation fosters goodwill and strengthens the bonds you have formed.

Seek Collaborative Opportunities: Look for opportunities to collaborate with individuals in your network. Joint projects or partnerships can create win-win situations, allowing you to combine strengths and achieve shared objectives. Collaboration deepens relationships and opens doors to new possibilities.

Be Mindful of Personal Branding: Cultivate a strong personal brand that aligns with your values and goals. Be intentional about how you present yourself online and offline. Your reputation and personal brand play a significant role in attracting meaningful connections and opportunities.

Stay Updated and Engaged: Stay informed about industry trends, news, and developments. Regularly engage with your network by sharing insights, articles, or relevant updates. Actively participate in discussions and contribute valuable information to position yourself as a knowledgeable resource.

Seek Feedback and Continuous Improvement: Request feedback from individuals in your network to gain insights into areas where you can improve. Act on constructive feedback to enhance your skills and grow both personally and professionally. Being open to feedback demonstrates a commitment to growth and self-improvement.

Foster Long-Term Relationships: Focus on building lasting relationships rather than solely pursuing short-term gains. Invest time and effort in nurturing your connections over the long term. Regularly check in with individuals, offer support, and celebrate their achievements. Strong relationships built on trust and mutual support can withstand the test of time and provide ongoing benefits.

Networking and relationship building should be approached with sincerity and a genuine interest in establishing meaningful connections. By following these strategies and maintaining an authentic and nurturing approach, you can expand your network, create valuable relationships, and open doors to new opportunities for personal and professional growth.

Remember that networking and relationship building are ongoing processes. It takes time and effort to cultivate meaningful connections. Be patient, persistent, and nurturing in your approach. By investing in building a strong network and fostering genuine relationships, you create a support system that can contribute significantly to your personal and professional success.

CHAPTER SEVEN

Investing in your own future

Ways to invest in yourself

Number one read for growth

To be honest, learning to read for growth is the most accessible thing you can do for long-term progress and investment in yourself. People do not read books because their teachers force them to read uninteresting novels, and they are put off by it. There is a link with homework, and truth be told, we all loathed having to do homework school actually made you hate the most precious self-investment tool out there the ideal technique to set up a reading habit is to read what you enjoy till you love to read.

Number two: interact with others, locate a mentor

Talk to a variety of individuals from all backgrounds and views. The more you expose yourself to diverse forms of thinking, the better you will understand the world around you. More often than not, people live in what we refer to as ideological bubbles. If you hang out with people who are very similar to you, they live near you, consume the same content as you, think the same way you do, and vote the same way you do, you're basically creating an echo chamber where your ideas are redirected back at you. The problem is that growth occurs only when you expose yourself to new concepts. In your quest to talk to interesting people, some of them will become guiding lights for your future; choose one of them to become your mentor. If you're looking to invest in yourself, finding a mentor who's open to guiding you through life is one of the best investments you can make. Growth occurs when you either assimilate newfound knowledge or the old one gets replaced by better ones.

Make friends is the third thing.

Your network of friends and contacts serves as both a personal and professional safety net. Now, as we've previously stated, your network directly affects your net worth. The higher the quality of your connections, the wealthier you are in life. However, networking is not only important for professional and financial reasons. What kind of life is it when you go through it all without sharing it with the people you care about? After all, other people's happiness becomes your happiness, and the person without friends is missing a significant piece of the puzzle. Invest in the thing we call life: good friendships. Depending on the situation, this can entail calling them right afterwards after finishing the book, investing money, or using other resources to maintain the friendship. If your friendships have waned, it's because no one made an effort to invest in the relationship, and as a result, neither party benefited.

The fourth one goes far.

This argument builds on the two preceding ones since, in our experience, as you go more, your perspective on the world changes in the most positive way. When someone travels by plane for ten hours, their entire perspective on life changes. Karma may be at play, or perhaps there are other educational conventions and traditions. This realization that there is an entire universe out there that has been going on for all time without knowing or caring that you exist is quite a huge milestone in one's trip since it makes you less self-centred as you go. Being a traveller rather than a tourist will help you learn more about the place you're visiting because you can never learn about a country in a Starbucks or McDonald's. Travel is one of the very few things that, when you spend money on it, makes you richer. You'll be richer if you accept the culture and let it define your identity.

Take courses to develop your talents at number five.

The best investment you can make in yourself is to learn new skills. New skills are upgrades to the quality of the outcomes you can expect from your life; they're like priceless tools that you can use. The best part about learning new skills is that no one can take them away from you, which is why we always advise learning the fundamentals rather than the newest flashy technique. You are actually purchasing time and expertise rather than the actual content. We have the following brutally honest opinion: Your life is cheap because you don't respect yourself enough. If you believe spending $15 on a book or $250 on a course is too much money, then you haven't reached the end of your trip. We have never been scared to spend money on items since we know they will continually add value to our lives because even just one concept from a course or book may make you tens of hundreds or thousands of dollars.

Sixth, grasp how to and genuinely implement health in your life.

People disregard their health when they are young because they do not realize that health neglect would result in a bill in the future. You know how we often talk about trading with the future for personal gain? Most people take away from the future and use that health in the present. The more you develop, the more you comprehend the value of excellent health and good sleep. The difference between running at 95% brain capacity and running on the fumes provided by Red Bull at 3:00 AM Spend time and money learning about nutrition and the body, and then spend time and money making sure you receive the full benefits of that knowledge.

Seventh, sell something.

This is a piece on the most useful methods to invest in yourself. Selling something is hands down one of the best ways to improve. This form of workout requires so many skills to come together that your progress is accelerated as a result. Selling is one of those essential talents, so we can go into great length about it. As with anything, the more you do it, the better you get at it. When you set a goal to sell something, you must determine what to sell, who to sell to, how to communicate with the potential buyer, and how to deliver and close the deal. All of these steps can be applied to other aspects of your life, which is why practicing selling is one of the best investments you can make in yourself.

The eighth: tip is to improve your surroundings.

This has two distinct advantages. One, time management, where you stop wasting time trying to figure out where everything is or what to do next, and two, efficiency growth Even if you don't live a minimalist lifestyle, having things organized is a concept that most young people find difficult. Well-organized spaces help you to accomplish more tasks more quickly. The bad news is that some people never get it out of their heads because they spend their entire lives living in a constant environment dominated by chaos. Happiness, success, and a sense of calm come as a result of you putting order in the chaos of the world. You can start by optimizing your immediate environment and then expand outward.

9th, teach something

If you want to master something, teach it to others. Teaching is a wonderful technique that we've used ourselves since it requires you to rationalize things in a way that others can understand and follow along. It's one of the things we despised the most in school.

Instead of studying formulas and word-by-word chapters, learning ends when you start memorizing. Understanding should be the goal of learning. When you teach someone something, it forces you to ensure that you have a good enough grasp on the subject so that you can pass on that knowledge. In the process, you gain a lot of value because the information you're teaching is cemented into the wisdom palace that is your brain.

Number ten: create a distinct income stream that is not reliant on you.

This is the only completely financial issue on this list, and while everything we discuss is tangentially related to money and leads to more money in the long term, the truth is that you will never be wealthy until you have several revenue streams. You can make money by working hard in your business or finding a high-paying employment, but wealth comes from outside of work. How much are you making if you're not working? The realization that you're probably not earning much outside of your immediate efforts should hit you like a ton of bricks. You're here because you want to know how to invest in yourself well invest your money so you don't have to work for money. The most crucial element is that it is not dependent on you to generate additional income; otherwise, you would just get another work. Here are three books we strongly recommend on this issue.

1. The 4-hour work week,

2. The $100 start-up, and

3. The pipeline parable Read all three to learn how to construct for yourself.

The eleventh: improve your image

Investing in yourself means giving you access to the most opportunities to get there. You'll have to give up the handstand keg chugs you and the boys did last summer that are all over the Internet. We all judge people by their appearances, we can't help it, and your social media profiles are the new emperor's clothes. If you think it doesn't affect you, you're probably lying to yourself. Purge your Facebook Clean up your LinkedIn profile, do some press, and possibilities will start to come your way. Now, start taking better care of yourself by learning about fitness, grooming, and personal hygiene, and the snowball will continue to roll in your favour.

The number twelve: Regularly expose oneself to art and innovative ideas.

Most people don't realize how valuable art is; they believe paintings are pricey, and who has time to look at statues, buildings, or prints when we have ATV celebrities to attack on Twitter? Creativity breeds value, and the only way to be creative is to exercise your creative muscle. Think of it like a light in a room: the more you expose yourself to others, the brighter yours shines. You connect the dots differently, and you learn about different approaches outside of family. Art should inspire you it should make you think it should make you question things it will tell you more about yourself that's why you should make a habit of coming face to face with creativity at every opportunity you get there are two great shows on Netflix which you should definitely watch if this sparked some interest in you one abstract the art of design phenomenal show which spoke to our creative side and two chefs table we're big foodies but their take on creativity.

The thirteenth learn a new language

Learning a new language has immediate marketplace added value you'll get better jobs or better deals because of it and that's not all when you're learning a new language your brain is expanding you're learning culture you're learning new structures which will all have recurring results over time and it doesn't hurt your inner circle increases in value because of your newfound passion going to a restaurant in Italy and ordering an Italian makes all of our Italian friends jealous.

Fourteen improved equipment and tools

Buy better tools that allow you to either increase the quality of your work or do your work faster early on in your journey at least 70% of your residual income should be reinvested in equipment that is directly correlated to bringing in more money why because these are things you only need to buy once and then you'll be good to go at some point you'll have everything you need and these tools will pay for themselves in the short to medium term don't be afraid to spend some more on things that make money not only are they our deductible expense but you can't afford to waste time fixing problems that can be solved by simply throwing money at them and finally.

The fifteenth Practice introspection and stop saying yes to everything

here's why introspection is one of the most valuable skills we've developed over the years it ties in with meditation but not only that we're all carrying a lot of baggage with us the goal of introspection is for you to solve the issues of the past one by one until one day when all you have to worry or stress about is the issues at hand This is a critical step toward happiness. Can you imagine getting to a point in your life where all of your worries boil down to simple and trivial things you should the additional step to this is not bringing in new issues some of you, and we're calling you out on this, say yes to things you know you don't want to do and people take advantage of that leading you to a more miserable life than you deserve Stop live for others and start thinking about what you want out of life for yourself. Investing in yourself entails taking all of the things we've stated seriously and pursuing them because you realize and can see the direct benefit and impact they have on your existence, which leads us to ask how many of these 15 you actually pursue.

Here it is invest time before you invest money until you have enough money to invest to buy time. This is one of those concepts that governed our lives for the better half of our professional lives growing up because we didn't have much to invest but we were all given the same amount of time so we put as much time as we could into the things that had the potential of getting us to the point where we could buy time with the money that we've made.

As a result of people's ignorance that you are actually purchasing time, you will find yourself perceived as having overpaid. Everyone loves to talk about the return on investment or even the return on time, but we want to pose the following question: everything we've discussed in this book is aimed to help you become more than you already are. Nobody can make you rich, fit, or brilliant; that is not their job. What's your return on investment? The more valuable you are as a person, the wiser and healthier you are because when all things come together, you are the one creating value. It is you who is generating the positive return on your life. It is your passion, hunger, and drive that you are channelling for change. If you've made it this far, we want to take advantage of the opportunity to spend money in yourself so that you won't have to invest time in measuring your influence.